In memory of Deirdre Green (24th September 1954–
6th March 1990): scholar, mystic, and friend.

And for Tony, with love.

*"When the transformation
comes, it will be sudden..."*

HILARY
LLEWELLYN
-WILLIAMS

Book of
Shadows

SEREN BOOKS

SEREN BOOKS is the book imprint of
Poetry Wales Press Ltd
Andmar House, Tondu Road, Bridgend, Mid Glamorgan

British Library Cataloguing in Publication Data
Llewellyn-Williams, Hilary
  Book of shadows.
  I. Title
  821.914

ISBN 1–85411–041–1

*The publisher acknowledges the financial support of the
Welsh Arts Council*

Cover Illustration: 'Bond of Union' by M.C. Escher
Lithograph, 1956, 25.3 x 33.9 cm
By kind permission of the Haags Gemeentemuseum

Typeset in 11 point Palatino by Megaron, Cardiff
Printed by John Penry Press, Swansea

Contents

Acknowledgements

With thanks to the Welsh Arts Council who provided financial assistance towards completing these poems; and to my family, for their support and good-humoured understanding while I was immersed in the byways of Renaissance occult philosophies.

Some of the poems have appeared in *The New Welsh Review*, *Planet*, *Poetry Review*, *Poetry Wales*, *Other Poetry*, *The PBS Anthology 1988*, the *National Poetry Competition Prizewinners Anthology 1986*, and *Exchanges - Poems by Women in Wales*.

TWO RIVERS

TO THE ISLANDS

Driving to Llanybydder from the hills
in sunlight, a clean blue sky
bathing us in its image: a light-pocket,
an open eye in all those weeks of rain,

we suddenly saw the sea in a strange place,
inland. We followed a new coast:
pale lucid water filled the low ground
to the west, and risen islands stood

netted with fields or thinly brushed
with trees, and shoreside cottages
whitewashed, perched over a harbour —
a landscape from the inner Hebrides

exact and stunning. Though of course we knew
it was only a trick of mist, sucked up
from unremarkable sodden earth, still
we cried out happily: "Look at the sea!"

So it shall be someday, when the polar ice
melts, and expanding oceans lift
over the land again. Sea licking
these hills into islands and promontories

the Teifi swallowed into a sea-loch
and lush farms drowned, and hill-farms turned
into fishermen's cottages. We could see
the future in a bowl of clear water,

seeing the present too, scrying the land
that is always there but mostly invisible —
the land's other face, the place where boats
put out from curved inlets, and green fields

tilt down to the sea; where eels thread
their way between tall hedges. Sun low
behind us, as far south as it will go
as we ran into the outer blurs of mist

and the islands vanished. Above, we sensed
the summer colour of sky without seeing it:
and, turning west, we crossed the plain grey river
in silence, like driving through water.

FEEDING THE BAT

At first it was a small cold palmful
a hunched and sorry scrap, clenched still
but for an infinitesimal buzz and tremble

as we passed it from hand to hand
half fearful that the buzzing might explode
into uncontrollable flight. So we found

a box, and a place by the stove, and scrounged
a spoonful of dogfood from the corner shop
and waited. When the scratching started

we crowded round to listen: it was alive!
Lifting it out, it seemed larger; it moved
its clever head from side to side, gave

delicate soundings. Two eyes, dark points of light
gleamed, not at all blind, and long questioning
fingers gripped mine. Whiskered like a cat

with a cat's silken cunning it consented
to be fed from the end of a stick, opened
a triangle mouth wide, and dipped and lunged

manoeuvering meatlumps in. Laughing, we squeezed
waterdrops onto its nose, to hear it sneeze
minute bat-sneezes, to watch the supple greedy

slip of a tongue flick the droplets down.
As it warmed, it got bolder, nipping our skin
with needle teeth, unfolding its tucked wings

turning its goblin face to the window, where
milky chilled spring daylight lured
it to sudden flight, skimming at head height

a strange slow flutter, followed by a whisper
of displaced air. Awaiting a change of weather
we hung it in a bag to sleep over the stairs

and roused it for feeding. After the second day
it arched its back to be stroked, and played
a biting game, neck stretched impossibly

backwards, slyly grinning. That evening, the sun
shone. We carried it in its bag to a vacant barn
by the river. It squealed as I left it there, long

angry squeals; but I was firm. I would not
be quite a witch yet, stroking and feeding a bat
my ears tuned to its music, swooping, flitting about —

though I lean out to the buoyant dusk, for all that.

YOUR CASTLE PICTURE

The sky comes right down to the ground
in your picture. And my eye's led
over scrawled grass to the castle,
solid and grey with its black slits,
its great dark ruined archways. You
have remembered a strange sight
of windows through the arch; they shine
deep blue in the crayoned shadows.

Tremendous — but is it right
that the sky should come down
all the way to the ground?
Last week, your sky was childish, high
and innocent, blue strip
at the top of the page, and white
air everywhere. I liked the way
the sun hung under it, with yellow
leggy rays. I liked the earth
swept safe beneath our feet. So
what's happened to bring the sky so low,
the earth so hunched and high?
The sun shrunk to a blurred smear
too bright to focus on?

I look at you, but your smile is clear colour,
glowing, unspoiled. There's a storm outside
blundering with charcoal clouds
I could almost paint. The sky
is close to us: it's scribbled on the ground.

Little son, as you ran shouting in the gale
I stuck your castle picture to my wall.

LIFE CLASS

Here is my arm. My weight rests
lightly, poised and yielding
to take the load of my body
while letting the blood flow;
so when the tingle begins I can
shift a little, imperceptibly
without spoiling your view of the lines
the angles and shadows.
I watch the texture of light
on the slopes of my arm, and regard
its landscape, as if for the first time.

Here are my legs. Doubled-up
my knees may present problems
of perspective. My thighs plunge
highlighted against the floor.
My trapped calves throb a little.
Soon the pain will start
to needle and stab, and I'll
breathe in rhythm, alongside,
keeping my distance.

Here is my stomach. There's a twist
in this posture, a challenge:
I am all changing planes.
The one part of me
that's visibly moving, rising
and falling as I breathe:
my belly, my centre
that cannot be still.

And my breasts, here, are just
two curves of light
and between my legs, a shadow.

Here is my head. I've tied
my hair so the stem of my neck
shows, the precise tilt,
the line between spine and brain.
I've turned my face aside
in abstraction. I prefer no
eye-contact: it jolts me back
into your world, the world
of touch and movement.
So I arrange my gaze
on a picture, a fragment of curtain,
two wood-knots, the flesh of my arm.

A long, slow time. The scratch
and shirr of pencils on paper
charcoal's thick squeak and whisper
clatter of brushes in water
subdued words, coughs and sighs
entertain me. I feed my mind
on all that concentration.

And yet it empties itself
constantly, it can't hold
to any thought, it must move —
or I can't keep still. It turns
and shifts, it is shrouded,
veiled: you can't draw it,

it's not available. My body
is public as the body of a tree
but my mind's private, goes
walkabout, darts like a bird.

Though there's one thought
returning, over and over.
How am I shameless
before strangers, before
their intimate gaze, yet
when my lover said, Stand up —
walk round the room; I want
to look at you — yes turn
like that... why did I blush
move stiffly, rapidly,
and cover myself with laughter?

MOVING THE BOXES

(for Anabel)

This was the least I could give you:
My strength on the far side of a box
Packed with your hidden life, the weight
Of cheerful clutter, our years apart.
Our backs and arms were strong
Together, making a dance of it.

I pushed the sides shut, and you taped
All joins and edges tight against time
And weather; our eyes met over the stacks,
We laughed a lot. You folded summer clothes
For a distant season. It was work, tough
Labour, pressing the grief right down.

It was the last I could give you:
A catkin branch from the river, a clutch
Of snowdrops, their white winged faces;
My scrubbing-out of cupboards, scratch
Meals from the ends of packets, a spread
Of coloured cards, chances, changes.

And for me, the gathering-up of love
Giving me heart again. We could see
Each other now quite clearly without our men:
Our perfect, matched movements, our double power.
It was no trouble. The boxes are well filled;
Now for the hard part. We'll share the load.

THROUGH THE WALLS

Old Jock is crying through the walls again.
Yesterday I saw him in his garden
bayoneting weeds
staking sweet peas to attention:
and then a slow fourth coat of paint to the fence.

He is lying on the carpet in his swept
parlour, a teacup smashed
at his side, and Missus sped
downhill to the telephone.
He murders his pain. His walls are red
tartan, Crawford colours, biscuit tins.

Last night, we heard them come in
from the club: the slam
of doors, his parade-ground yell.
We sniggered under bedclothes, listening.
Inches from our heads
his teenage son sobbed, sobbed
as Jock ran out in the street, hurling dark
obscenities after the grown one.
Missus begged peace,
made tea and sandwiches as the moon set.

"They wrote me off" he said, and his false teeth
clamped on a smile; "but I'm a bonny fighter."
His eyes were wild blue, the pupils ringed
with death. "I canna eat
since they cut the guts from me" — but he wolfed
his biscuits, chewed soft white bread.
Missus takes care of him. The heavy smell
of mutton cloys our cupboards.

"Did you hear him scream?" she asked me
last time, rosy with pride. And now
there's a crash of falling chairs, and the ragged shouts
of battle. Soon an ambulance will stop
outside, to a flicker of curtains.

An enemy cat prowls in the drill lines
of his borders. I watch the wall.

A CONCERT OF CHINESE MUSIC

ON RADIO THREE

rare, delicious sun
mingles with the water-notes
of a Chinese flute

frost on the windows
disassembling its fronds
gently, easily

to a sound of gongs
the Dragon of Spring set loose
on Khingan mountain

in these cold Welsh hills
I call a five-pointed scale
and watch the sun come

HOUSE

I will live in a House
By the Side of the Road
& Be a Friend to Man
(John Crowley: *Little, Big*)

House of irregular stones
House of sparkling quartz fragments
House roofed with split slate

Low house backed onto a wet field
With a generous yellow door
A cobbled yard studded with dandelions
And in winter, stacked with cut logs

House in the flightpath of gales
House blown about with mist
House with the wind in its walls

A cramped untidy house, dark
As a shed with a view
Of great western cloudscapes
The voice of December in its broad chimney

House forged in primal fire
House of resinous flame
House whose stones store summer

Whose narrow windows catch the slow
Movement of sun along the ridge
The slide across seasons, the shift
Of light on our faces each morning

House polished by rain
House of brimming gutters
House with its roots in water

Its floorstones shaped in a river
Scud of ripples on their washed faces
House shod with fossil mud and waveprints
Wading through water like a stone ship

House of uneven timbers
House of broad ancient planks
House that creaks in the wind

Its ceiling beams filched from a wrecked vessel
Its oak lintels bowed with the weight of years
Sawdust trodden into the hall carpet
And woodsmoke heavy in the furnishings:

Though its windows are deep and small
They show us an immensity of stars
And the stars seem small from our immensity
And time a poem made in the walls of a house.

UNDER EAVES WOOD

night still crouched, and the track
fell steeply into shadow.
We followed, our minds full of sleep

but our feet exact and sure
over mud and black stone outcrops.
Below, the brimming trough

of the valley, starred with lights;
and ahead, a slim moon
burned and tilted in infinity.

Two figures hurrying through dawn
under the weight of the hills, the trees'
crowded terrace, not looking

but feeling their way through
the wood's still life. The air
was charged; it sparked with hope

the cool blue tingle of a good day.
My bag bumped at my shoulder. You moved
before me, swift as a cat

through the open door of morning.
For each of us, without judgement,
Eve's blessing on our path, our way.

TWO RIVERS

It was here, in the long red meadow
two princes fought a battle
in old times, in the shadow
beneath this hill
in this dark sorrel
where children roll and squeal
flattening pathways in the brushed grass.
This ridge, the high seat
its flank woods heavy with summer —
was this where he raised his spear,
stood lightly rehearsing the blow

while the villagers swarmed below
with pop and crisps and bright-striped folding
chairs, men in tweed caps, women
in pale blue nylon housecoats
faces pink in an unaccustomed sun?

And the one they fought for — was she
there in the crowd with her schoolfriends
pressed round her, craning for a sight
of blood? Or sitting high
as a bird, like a Carnival Queen?
Or did she stand alone with her hair down,
her fingers twisting together, down by the river
to her knees in plumes of meadowsweet?

I think she turned her face when the blow fell
and the crowd yelled and horns blared
towards the place where the two rivers meet.

Two rivers, brown and muscled, struggle
endlessly in a pool. Warm afternoons
in our own short summer, I've gone there
to skinny-dip, the shock
of water raising up gooseflesh.
Feeling the two floods not quite equally cold:
    one with a little sun in it
    one with the mountain in it
and my body between the two
touching them both, as she once used to do.

Was it here, to this shadowed pool
when the show was over
she fled with her nine maidens
pursued by redfaced men, her triumphant lover?
Along the footpath from the post office
they ran to fetch her; but she'd flown
with her white turned face into the alder scrub
in a flurry of wings and claws.

Now they have lost her in the long
meadow; and their darkness is complete.

She flies high
here, in the woods, at night —
I've heard her thin cry, where the rivers meet.

A WORLD ELSEWHERE

My daughter stood in the sunlight, winnowing grain.
I sat at her feet, looked upwards: she was strong
astride in her blue dress, her forearms busy.
The chaff scattered, sailing down to me
on the threshing-floor. A hilltop breeze
ruffled in through the doors, from the world
of summer. Her youngest daughter curled
asleep on my lap, dark in my nestled crook.

Chaff coming down like light; the rattling grain
in its round skin tray; and a sound
of singing from the hill. Such a strong blue
sky out there: in here, a gold sifting.
The barley-smell. Smell of my daughter's sweat.
Warm weight of the child against my bones.

I sat in moving shadows, and I laughed:
throaty, low — an old woman's privilege.
Throaty, low, in the dusty winnowing,
the floating husk, sun motes. To think
of all we'd journeyed through! Of how
I'd carried them with me, children and seeds
of children, through years of horror, to arrive
here. Through poison, cold and hunger, through
the infected City, blood and guns, despair
to arrive here. Above, the wide circle
of shaking grain. Outside, cut straws
in an August sun. Birch saplings starting up
from the ruins of a town. My grandchildren.

She turned to look at me. "There's loads to do
Mum, and you sit there cackling."
The small girl shifted, opened a brown eye slowly.
My daughter, cooling in her blue dress, smiled.

BRYNBERLLAN

This is a place where nothing really grows
but water: water and stones.

And concrete bungalows, and lost holdings.

Tilt of water from the mountainside
pushes under the road, and stones grow
overnight in our gardens: rainbuffed hard
perennials. We're on the flank
of the wind, even in summer.

But years ago, this was an apple orchard.

Rows and patterns of trees, all the way
down to the stream called *Comely*;
mossy barked, their darkblue stems at dusk,
the sun spread white at dawn on slopes
of blossom; warm air, stirred thick
with honey. Humming and swarms, and then
the smell of ripe fruit: those small
sharp western apples.

Crowded faces, bushels and basketfuls.

Everyone there, at work in the branches,
measuring the loads, brownarmed
and busy. Shouts in the crisp leaves.
Children rolling windfalls down the hill.
Foxes nosing at night through bruised grass.

And apple smoking in the soul-fires.

I think the traffic worsens year by year
just passing through. Rain's harsher too:
laced with acid and caesium, it fills
the stream called *Comely* and the stream
called *Blossom*. Nothing flourishes.

Yet sometimes we'll distill, between breath

and breath, a taste of sweetness:
yes, even now, a rustling of leaves
a blossom-drift. Between low flakes
of October sunlight, treeshapes flicker;
and evenings to the West bring cloud-landscapes
rising like a range of wooded hills,
a place of apple-orchards. Not here: beyond

reach, elsewhere, forsaken, forfeited.

LLANTHONY PRIORY

It's a heathen rain today
driving over the high pass from Hay
falling in blown webs and torn shreds
over great weights and sacred elevations
raised to withstand the weathers of the world
now letting the wet world in;

falling on arches propping up the wind
falling on these stumps of sure foundation
falling in smoke-drift down the long nave
falling like a shaken benediction

over the damp chancel and shattered tower
over the drip, drip in the canons' kitchen
over the lost cloister and buried choir:

an irreligious rain. We stand in its lee
by a bit of stacked buttress.

Geese in a little paddock stuck with trees
stretch their rude necks at us. My children
yelling and running down the green slope
of the altar steps, chase round the sanctuary.
And in the prior's lodging, yellow elder
waggles her sexy fruits.

The ruins shape our gaze; they lift
our eyes to the hills: from whence cometh rain.
The immanent and omnipresent hills
which were always there, during lauds and vespers
a mighty unseen eminence, like God

waiting beyond the walls. And now
they've broken through that careful masonry
in a pantheon, tremendously circled,
splendidly photogenic, framed in stone.

I lift my camera, and wander round
to capture an alignment. Dewi's rain
gusts down from Wales, floating in fine drops
in your pagan hair. Our Lady pours
dark red in rivers from the mountainside
chanting perpetual sorrows. Holy wells
are rising. Litanies and psalms
from vivid, potent, scarlet tongues of bracken.

These sharpedged, lovely lines
are spare and windswept, leave us comfortless.
You huddle in your coat. Let's go back soon,
and sample the real ale at the Half Moon.

THE LITTLE CLOTH

The odour of sanctity. Candles
their clear warm waxy spirits,
fresh cut blooms in paschal yellows and white,
bitter incense swung by a solemn boy,
the smell of washed Sunday bodies.

I was fifteen: I had waited a long time.

I knelt between mother and sister.
The priest moved his hands like a doll
decked out in ivory and gold for Easter.
Latin today: charmed occult syllables
long rustling silences, the soft chink of censers,
altar boys, white lace, male mysteries.

Sleepily I watched my own candle dip
and shrink in its fiery terrace
under the virgin's peeling plaster toes.
I hugged an unusual dragging ache, a tightness.

Sometimes I thought I might become a saint
to go into ecstasy and talk with angels;
not worry about my figure, my crop of spots
but to live in a forest hut on wild herbs
breathing wisdom like clean air.

The bell's small icy note
startled me back: the white moon
of the host raised up, then the chalice.
This is my blood, he said, and drank,
and wiped the cup. When that cloth is washed

(a priest once told me) the woman
must be in a state of grace
and the water not tipped down the sink
but emptied on the ground — just think of it.

My grandmother washed and washed little bloody cloths.

Ecce Panis Angelorum a woman sang
from the choir, her voice sexless and pure.
Strong vowels responded: I felt a loosing
of knots, a moist unfolding
from darkness, my chalice filled with blood

and the gold eyes of every angel turned
towards me, and I burned
with sudden grace, and my moon-Jesus rose
from the shadows and saw me. I was a saint at last —
my blood poured out for you
and for many; my new huge pride.

The soft white secret cloth
between my legs, reminded me all day.

A NORTHWEST PASSAGE

A recent autopsy on the bodies of three of the members of Lord
Franklin's last expedition revealed that they died of lead poisoning
from contaminated tinned food.

Franklin's seaman lies in a dream of ice:
his brain's turned into an oval lump
of solid ice. It fills
his skull with a cloudy whiteness.

His body is unchanging, six feet
down in the permafrost. He has forgotten
sunlight through green leaves,
tartness of orchard apples, the warm
loam of Kent. In his cells
an Arctic silence. His last thoughts frozen.

What made them sew him up
warmly in all his shirts? Was it
to keep him from the cold?
Why did they struggle with clumsy picks
ringing on frozen gravel, hour after hour
in shrieking winter darkness
chipping and spitting ice, to make graves?

Was it love, in that awful place?

This decent, graceful gift:
a red cloth laid like a prayer
over his face, hiding the terrible clamp
of pain, the lips drawn back
over uneven teeth, the eyes locked.
Too tall for the hasty coffin, they crammed him in
with one arm twisted beneath him.

John Torrington, John Hartnell, William Braine:
abandoned with their chiselled names
in a dead time, poison in their bones
and guts, and hair. In Arctic time

the wind is a true presence:
the sky is the world
surrounding a small circle of shifting ice.

And the names of the trapped ships
Terror and *Erebus*
are a dreadful presence; and the names
of Franklin and his crew
dragging the weight of a slow death
blindly over the snow, daft wanderers
searching for a way through

stumbling into the sun, are a presence.

THE SEALWIFE

One day I shall find my skin again:
my own salt skin, folded dark, its fishweed stink
and tang, its thick warm fat, great thrusting tail

all mine: and I'll take it and shake it out
to the wind, draw it over me cool and snug,
laugh softly, and slip back to my element.

I shall find my stolen skin, hidden by you
for love (you said) that night the sea-people danced,
stashed in some cleft in the rocks where I may not go

but used to go, and dance too, stepping free
in my new peeled body, the stalks of my legs in the moonlight strange, my long arms shaping the sky

that have narrowed their circles down
to the tasks of these forked hands: lifting,
fetching, stirring, scrubbing, embracing — the small

stiff landlocked movements. In the sea
I plunged and swam for my own joy, sleek and oiled,
and I loved at will in rolling-belly tides.

Here love is trapped between the walls of a house
and in your voice and eyes, our children's cries;
whose boundaries I've understood, a language

learnt slowly, word by word. You've been dear and good —
how you would sing to me, those wild nights!
—and oil my breasts by firelight, and dip down

to taste my sea-fluids. I'd forget to mourn
those others then, trawling the flickering deeps.
Now I cry for no reason, and dream of seals:

an ocean booms in the far cave of my ear
and voices tug at me as I stand here
at the window, listening. Our children sleep

and by daylight they run from me. Their legs
strong, their backs straight, bodies at ease
on solid ground — though they play for hours on the shore

between sand and sea, and scramble the wet rocks
gladly. It won't be long now, the waiting:
they love to poke and forage in the cracks

of the cliffs; sharpeyed, calling, waving.

THE BEE-FLIGHT

That was a strange, rare place, in a loop
between river and nippled hill
with a crooked sandstone church and trees
that corkscrewed, and a massive leaning yew
one thousand years thick, peeled rosy flesh
and a woman carved into the north wall
with legs agape, and a man with a bird's head
whistling sorcery. The ground rose
in hummocks: the past, carelessly buried,
trying to break through. Snowdrops showed white
and wet below the mound. I stood at the cusp
of spring in a flayed landscape
bleached-out by frost, stripped clean

as an old bone, sucked dry. I'd thought
there was nothing to fill me, nothing to speak to me;
but here was rain smelling of turned earth,
the sun in watercolour, curved paths,
storybook trees, bark swirled, bulged-out and fissured
peopling the place. At the edge of a pool
a straddled oak with a hole
at eye level, forced me to stare. Birds calling, then
a humming past my ear, and again; brown bees
sailing in from the sedges, dipping down
into darkness, hollow mouth-oak, in and in
with grains of new gold. A ragged shower blew
up from the west. Something unfolding, stirring

under my feet. The lumpy, breast-topped crag
now spiralled in light; the birdman suddenly answered
by choruses of wings, and the opened thighs
of the sandstone witch by the presence of flying bees.

BREAKFAST WITH THE POETS

Dawn at the Alcazaba.
The poets come
up from the drowsy city, appearing like birds
from a woven nest of alleys
some walking, most in cars
turning difficult corners in the dark
all drawn to the honey rock

in scores, in hundreds
from under stones, on a breeze from the desert,
the folds of the sea. They've come
with spouses, friends and children, greeting
each other on the steps of the citadel
of light. That woman in evening dress
hasn't slept all night. That child,
like ours, stares through us,
eyes blank with dreams. They climb
and we climb with them
through the sultan's exquisite garden
shaping word after word.

Up in the high courtyard
are men with microphones, women
trailing long veils. Everyone laughs, delighted.
We lean together over rose-coloured walls
and watch the sun
rise over stripped hills, ruined terraces.
This is a strange country
breeding poets instead of flies. They swarm
in the pure, steady light.

They hand out dazzling blankets:
like loaves and fishes, it's a miracle —
everyone sits down. Music swells
in a wild, muezzin cry.
A woman lifts brown arms, releasing
a pigeon. *See, I have laid*
my greeting in the collar of a dove
which will fly over the land
of Almería like a flung censer.

The poets read in turn
women and men, intensely
darkly and gloriously. Children wriggle:
I can't understand
all the words either; but they seem
poems of celebration.

Morning expands and blazes; the sun hits
the wall above us with a gold fist.
The city is awake: it roars
and glitters in wilderness; a bucket
of whitewash thrown at the mountains.
Comrade poets, ladies, gentlemen,
now breakfast will be served:
herb tea and spicecakes in the high tower
of Ibn Al-Mu'tasim.

ANDARAX

(Almería, Andalusia)

On the map, a broad blue sinuous line said
water. Dark, fluid and cool
from the snows of Sierra Nevada,
bordered by orange groves and thirsty vines
threading and falling, a ripple between banks

because in Wales a river means moving water
I pictured that. So nothing prepared me for
nothing — that yawning ditch of dust,
that void, that absence. Sun spat
and crackled in the stones. Baked mud

cracked open. A long bridge spanned
the gulf. Everything the bleached-out dun
of old shit. On a ruinous site nearby
a JCB dug slowly: the dust went ten feet down —
further, the whole way. Crossing the no-river,

crossing the Andarax, I shuddered; my throat
dry as a lizard's, my eyes peeled raw.
Down to bedrock. Even its name's a cough,
a rasp, a drought. It does not summon liquid,
shadowy pools, slack shallows, slide of fish.

It's the name of a slaughtered dragon;
a mythical beast; a fossil; a chained Book
of Spells, with dark parchment pages: *Andarax*.
Somebody mentioned a winter legend of water,
snow-floods. I could not believe it:

that was too long ago, in another country.

BOOK OF SHADOWS

"Because ideas are the basic forms of things, according to which everything is made...we should create in ourselves the shadows of ideas...in order to shape them to all possible realities. We create them in us, images revolving like wheels. If you know any other way, try it."

(Giordano Bruno: *On the Shadows of Ideas* [Paris, 1582])

"Doctor Jordano Bruno Nolano, a professor in philosophy, intends to pass into England; whose religion I cannot commend."

(Henry Cobham, English Ambassador in Paris, 1583)

To Begin With....

The shadows of ideas are the stuff of poetry. They are the symbols and metaphors we use to express reality: they are language itself, in which each word is a symbol, the shadow of an idea, a *spell* by which we gain some power in the world, able to shape our will and direct it.

Four hundred years ago the connection between poetry and magic was more directly understood than it is today. The power of words to change lives was respected and feared. Our ancestors also understood the importance of imagery, the ability to directly visualise a memory or an idea, in order to make it real. So dreams could be turned to reality, ideas could begin to affect the external world. And the mysterious and awesome powers that controlled the Universe and the workings of Nature could, they believed, be drawn into oneself and used.

Such were the dreams and ideas behind a fantastic outpouring of creativity in the European Renaissance. That belief in the power of human imagination to change the world, the excitement of rediscovering a mythical golden age of wisdom and looking forward to a visionary future, a new age, was the driving force behind the great paintings and music, architecture and literature of those times.

When the new ideas challenged the status quo too directly, their expounders were likely to get burned. Such a free-thinker who met with a grisly end was the 16th century philosopher, magician and poet Giordano Bruno. It was only to be expected: not only did he claim that the earth and the whole of Nature was alive and divine, not only did he propose that the earth moved around the sun in a boundless universe of suns and worlds, but he predicted the fall of the Christian order and its replacement with a new religion based on a revival of paganism: the 'Religion of the World'.

You can read more about Bruno and his ideas in the Notes at the end of this book. His vision and his character are the impetus behind this sequence of poems; the poems are my response from our own times of change. They are not really about Giordano Bruno and the

16th century — many better and factual books have been written about that. Although Bruno appears here, I must stress again: these poems are not about him.

They are about us.

They are about the world we live in now, and the issues we face now; which, strangely enough, are the same old issues, but differently dressed.

Occasionally Bruno may appear to take centre stage, speaking in his own voice, and several poems turn on incidents in his life. Other poems are more directly in my own voice; while others are deliberately ambiguous. I am not writing about history, but about what concerns us all: the world we live in, our environment — physical, spiritual, emotional.

Moving through the coded rich symbolism of the Tarot Trumps, I link Bruno's archaic worldview with our own, and discover strange parallels. I explore the old relationship between poetry and magic, and between magic and love, and understand that it has never been broken.

HLW Pencader 1989

O

NOLA

In my childhood, I though nothing existed beyond Vesuvius
(*De Immenso*)

Now I understand, I understand everything.
Bird's eggs are small pieces of sky;
the chicks inside are stolen from the wind

and the wind blows because the trees move it
with their dancing leaves: they move the lake too
into waves. And I know where night is made:

in the lake, from black stones in the mud there.
Dark breathes out and rises from the water,
and daylight every morning moves the leaves.

In those trees by the river, mothers find their babies;
I've seen them walking into the woods with baskets
on windy afternoons. Today I helped Mamma

pick bilberries. She said I'm sharp as a bird.
I know about angels, too: they live in the Sun,
but they visit Nola sometimes secretly

streaming down in bars of light — they look like specks
but they're really huge, huge. Here's my cave
where I talk to them, and leave them figs and flowers:

in the morning there's nothing left, so I know they love me.
Can you see that dark hump where the world ends?
We call it Vesuvius, the shadow mountain;

nobody lives there, it's too black and cold —
not like our green mountain, with goats and sheep
and Uncle Taddeo's hut, and the white track

up to the summer pasture. There's our holy well
with its chained cup, and light in the water
rolling around like a snake to make you strong.

And I have discovered bee-swarms in the earth:
I've heard them when I lie in the June grass
on hot still days, humming under my head,

under my hands, down in the earth's hive —
or is it the world buzzing? That deep, thick honey voice,
her soil, her stones, alive. See! I understand.

I

BOOK OF SHADOWS

Behold now, before you, the man who has pierced the air and
penetrated the sky, journeyed among the stars and soared beyond
the margins of the world...   (*La Cena dei Ceneri*)

Under the shadow of the good and true
I am feeling, groping my way through an inner room
a mole in a mass of roots, no a fish among weeds
seeing and touching in silence by greenshift sun.
Holding it all, holding it all together:
gathering up, mending the smashed mirror
seven-thousand-years' bad luck; and here's the one
clear perfect image, the crazed world newly reflected
turning in unison, its scattered notes
tumbling into a song — now then, hold on
to that mirror image — building, joining-up
atom to atom in the universe
in a great golden chain. The bee flies out

from its close monastic cell, never having seen
flowers, but having an image of flowers
somewhere imprinted, sees and smells and knows
the source of sweetness, burrowing with joy
and bringing treasure home. I am a bee.
The different colours of flowers do not confuse me.

So I make, comb by comb, my magic book —
a Book of Shadows. Its pages flicker and gleam
as if seen underwater; its letters red and black,
its curious diagrams, mad conjurations
scud in and out of light, unreadable.
But as I draw it slowly from the pool

of Imagination, look! It becomes plain, easy.
This is magic; what I do. I have come to you
with the world up my sleeve and heaven in my hat
shuffling a clutch of pictures. On my pied robe
I've sewn the stars invisible: they are inside,
within, where they should be — Luna and Sol,
Mercury, Bootes, the Bull, the Banquet.

Now shut your eyes. I can make you see them too:
stars in a meadow, knuckles on a tree,
galaxy shells, lost cities at low tide
shouldering out of the slime. Hold it all, all
precious and rare, mind-mirror, dazzling round
Book of infinite pages, colours, shadows and sound.

II

ATHENE

Her have I loved and sought from my youth, and desired for my spouse, and have become a lover of her form...and I prayed...that she might be sent to abide with me, that I might know what I lacked...for she knew and understood...   (*Oratio Valedictoria*)

First, they made me an eye.
In the cold revolving stars, in the storm,
in the flying sun, in the place where water
comes out of the earth, an eye.
The eye watched; they were not alone.
They scratched its shape on stones
where the dead lay. Its rays spun out
weblike, encompassing the world;
drilled into bone, a passage, a way through.

Next, they made me a brow.
Over two staring circles, a double bow,
thick plunging curves, a look
of intense concentration. Life
with some thought behind it, an intelligence.
By now, they'd invented pots:
comfortable pregnant bellies, with twin eyes
frowning out of the clay. Sense
out of nonsense. Room to grow.

Then came the owl: that was natural.
Something alive and searching after dark —
that great dished listening face.
Soundless flight; wings a whisper of snow,
then the sudden swoop of death.

The voice of a world both fearful and beautiful
was a shuddering *hoo, hoo.* That suited me.
I flew secretly; I stunned, I wooed,
I tore apart, I saw and heard all.

And lastly, a woman born
out of sea-foam, out of flowers, or from
the head of a god — ridiculous. I'd been
too generous: the people thought too much;
they gorged on metaphors, they killed for them.
I was Athene, wise and terrible
flinging my spears, helmetted with the Moon,
crowned with stars, a woman clothed with the Sun
defending Right and Might and Truth and Freedom.

But now, little monk, by dusk
I see you kneeling on the cold flags
of your narrow cell, and your mind
is all eyes. In your heart a dark fire,
a lust. You have trusted me
and I have come: but I will not come kind
or maidenly — never forget, I am taloned,
banished from daylight, savage with desire —
but beautiful, yes my love; and I see, I see.

III

THE INNER ARTIFICER

Man labours on the surface of things; but Nature works from within.
(De Causa)

The scientist's posed in a pigsty —
an awkward smile on his round foolish face —
with his creature, transgenic monster, poor pig,
blind, bloated and arthritic, a coarse slab.
That smile of hesitant triumph,
those well-scrubbed fingers touching the prone
thick body in the straw, show no remorse;
more a coy, teasing promise, an allure.

And I wonder, Bruno, what you'd think of him
that gene-magician in his white coat,
his surface-work. They still say *Mother Nature* —
meaning a woman, weak and pliable,
limited, passive, open to be explored,
discarded, raped. Mother gives more and more.

But among us, *da noi*, Nature is called
the inner artificer. And she's everywhere,
strong, steadfast: power in the womb
of matter, the spirit that shines
through things. She's a voice
heard in a room, sounding to each corner,
everywhere resonant; we can't turn from her.

And she returns us our filth, feeds us
our stored-up poison. She will not spare
the seals, or our children. Deserts balloon,

malignant. As we divide, negate,
reduce and separate, she multiplies,
joins and reshapes the world, swarms out
from the core. She is not sentimental.

This grinning alchemist plays with the parts,
blind to the whole. Like his pig
he is paralyzed, stuck, sterile. He believes
in the old, flat, static Earth. He believes in Hell.

While Nature still works from her centre,
expelling galaxies, singing through every door.
Revolutionary Queen of the chromosomes,
the inner artificer. Hidden and sure.

IV

CONJURATION

Why, I say, do so few understand and apprehend the internal
power? ...He who sees all things, is all things.

(*De Imaginum Compositione*)

I draw into myself
The scarlet in this star,
The Fire that shaped the world,
All instruments of war

Heart's blood, birth-blood, stain
Of sun in a dawn sky,
Red banners blowing west
Wiping out tyranny:

I draw into myself
The green in this great wood,
The dark flood of the sea
April in blade and shoot

And breathe in liquid gold
Cold-running through my veins:
Power in the tiger's eye
Power in a storm of change

Breaking concentric spheres
Blowing from town to town
Oak-crowned, the Thunderer
Guarding the Gate of Horn

While a red-bearded King
Turns in his sleep of stone —
Ready for anything
I face this world alone.

I draw into myself
The Dragon, and the Sun;
Watchful, invincible,
My Destiny begun.

V

THE ART OF MEMORY

To understand is to speculate with images.
(*De Imaginum, Signorum et Idearum Compositionae*)

The sun blesses my face. I breathe
in its warm yellow strength. Stock-doves
play hollow flutes above me.
I close my eyes, assemble for a journey.

Frater Jordanus, whom you will observe
on the stone seat by the bay-tree, gazing inwards
at innumerable worlds, is our chief treasure;
a golden chestful, a dragon's hoard
of secrets. When his dark eyes turn
towards you, it's like falling into a well
that empties into night. And then there's that
slow, curved smile. Ask him:
he'll offer you jewels — he is generous,
though careful of course, as we all are,
knowing forbidden things. He stands at the brink
of a revelation, the winds of all time in his face,
his mop of hair. No, we don't yet know
what he's discovered; but he cultivates
                    our Art of Memory.

Now I build a castle on a hilltop
crowded with white towers.
In every room a thousand new spaces
that I shall fill with subtle images.
And every image wears its secret meaning:
something stupendous, unforgettable,
there, in its own place. That gives me power.

The brothers come to him, and certain books
pass from sleeve to sleeve. I think you know
what I refer to. Jordanus made our name
glorious here: the Holy Father
Himself received instruction. So you see
our problem — where to draw the line
between grace and heresy. Such brilliance,
such rainbow facets; we are all transfixed.
And this is why I point him out to you —
remember him. Sadly, he must be silenced.
A man who holds all heaven in his head
            cannot live long.

> *I know a double picture:*
> *the world of senses, and the world*
> *of image. That is my strength,*
> *my poetry, my secret. I have flown*
> *over the stars, and found no barrier,*
> *only more stars, more worlds.*
> *So listen, listen: we are all free,*
> *we cannot be walled in;*
> *not while we keep our Art of Memory,*
> *storehouse of truth, star-garden.*
> *Tremendous is the force*
> *of my spiritual intentions;*
> *empowering the message that I bear.*
> *Stop me, old men, if you dare.*

VI

HEROIC FRENZY

Is it for me to oppose the sacred order of Nature?...I have never
had a desire to become a eunuch. On the contrary, I should be
ashamed to yield on that score, were it only by a hair, to any man,
in order to serve Nature and God...
(*De Gli Eroici Furori:* preface addressed to Sir Philip Sidney)

In dawn light, Benedetta, your hair
tumbled over the pillow is darker
than resinous darkness from a cypress wood
where night still huddles; darker
than my blackest thoughts. When the sun floods
the window, you shall be brushed with copper,
ablaze with deep bronze. Here I rest my hand
on the sleeping curve of your spine, and over
the treasure of your breast, and my heart burns
with a small, secret fire. I won't forget
how I knelt to you last night, and offered homage
wordlessly, as you stood over me
shuddering in your joy. This, too,
is serving God and Nature: our splendid labour.

Waking before dawn, in my old way —
one habit I'll never lose — my morning prayer
is buried in your breathing. May it grow
inside you like a tree of white flowers
resplendent in a garden. I have come late
to this rule, this discipline, this new devotion:
forgive me, Benedetta. My life's path
is already chosen — work and loneliness.
I'm an explorer, bound for strange lands,
searching for what was lost; a buccaneer

with a price on my head; a danger. The sun
creeps up: your spread hair glows. Oh love
the choice is hard. I am a standing flame,
a bird in your hands. Hoist me high: let me go.

VII

THE JOURNEY

Any horizon, however extensive, suggests a beyond. (*De Immenso*)

Setting out again, taking the road again
that leads to some new city
    Adocentyn
or, for the time, Geneva, Avignon,
Toulouse or fabled London; setting out
in the dark, on a purseful of whispers —
go there, take this, speak to that man
who bears the sign we know of — hurriedly
fastening the points of my long hose
    seeming natural to me now

abandoning these streets, these squares
these clever, spiced gardens; in my heart
    a vow to return
and a lifting spirit, a joy
taking flight, driving me on.
I shall wheel round and round
this world like a Moon, like a comet
    leaving a fiery trail

never resting until I have seen
the City of Light accomplished
and all my friends safely installed therein
gathered from here and there. With this dream
I fill spare moments waiting in the rain
for promised horses, or a weary trudge
across town after an absent-minded fool:
    all the loose, empty hours

between me and my destination. Tonight
the sky is plunged thick with stars
my wild companions, hurtling with me
to an unknown end; which doesn't matter —
only the journey matters. I breathe
clean mountain air: a vision
of Nola brushes past. *Adocentyn.*
Perfect place, place that never was
nor shall be ever, compels me.
No end, then, to the dizzy Universe,
     no end to my journeying.

VIII

SUN IN LEO

...You see, then, how one simple divinity which is in all things, one fecund nature, mother and perserver of the Universe, shines forth in different subjects and takes different names ...Thus we should think of Sol as being in a crocus, a daffodil, a sunflower, in the cock, in the lion...   (*Lo Spaccio della Bestia Trionfante*)

Brazen summer, summer burnished and bold;
the sun exalted, the sky's hot copper
scalding our eyes, a tingle on the skin

and noon like a ringing of horns
in the hills, like a hammered coin.
The roadside leaves are dusty

and glittering. Between here and the coast
acres of sunflowers turn their polished heads:
gold worshipping gold. Their hearts

are rich oil. They thrust
from cool nourishing darkness into light.
At a low whitewashed house a woman stands

framed in her doorway: by her feet
two cats, one pied, one ginger.
Her hands supporting the jambs

hold the house steady as she gazes
beyond the blazing molten faces
of the flowers, beyond the dug rock

to where the lions are. They flow and circle
on a hot yellow plain, always moving
a little nearer through the dry grass,

muscles woven under satin skin;
their eyes half-closed and gleaming.
Lions moving together, coming at last

to the streets of the city, broad paws
and heavy shoulders spilling round corners
around parked cars, stepping down alleys

staring through windows with their gold eyes.
A stink of beast. The terrible roaring.
Everyone cowering behind locked doors

except one dark child, running out to them.
The woman lifts an arm
and rubs her forehead dry. Sweat stings

the rim of her lids. The cats
stretch and roll, stretch and roll,
greedy for sun. She tells them: It is done.

IX

IN AEGYPT

That which leads us to truth...is a kind of divine ignorance, together with disdain of the paths we have travelled, for it comes from that region towards which every path disappears...

(Eroici Furori)

I have forgotten how I arrived here.
The path is swallowed up
in mist from the mountains.
So much walking after dark, always alone.

Now, suddenly, the sun has found me
in a new country; though I've seen
it in dreams. It's shaken out
below the hill in its acres

shining with inward colours. *Oh
Aegypt, Aegypt, there will remain
of thy religion only fantasy —*
we work on what has been spoiled.

But look: you too, drawing near,
coming my way, stumbling over stones.
Come close, closer; your nearness
can't hurt me now. If I could

I'd give you a word-map of this territory:
but my words have become air.
So I stand with my heart and my hands bare
waiting for you to tilt your head, and see me.

And here's a secret: we've been here before
the quick way, at the gulf
of darkness, that furthest place
only found at the point of bliss, letting go

and tumbling out backwards into space
before the body kicks us into life
helpless, ecstatic, wild.
Last time, my limbs ached

for days from that journey.
So listen, and I'll tell you a mystery —
anything that's outside this unity,
soul of the world, is nothing.

We are all linked, all joined,
all travelling. You say
I can teach you something strange,
something unguessed, hidden

eyes, voices in the leaves. Oh yes,
yes, it's all there, alive, aware:
but you know it. All those unspoken questions
unfolding warm surprising impulses

those fleeting corner-visions, unborn
poems — they are within you; all
the answers. But just ask me anything,
take my hand, follow. This is your country too.

X

THE REVOLVING CASTLE

The Infinite Universe moves in circles...like the turning of a wheel;
which remains motionless in itself while all its parts are moving.
(Eroici Furori)

The small spiders of spring weave webs of spun droplets
catching newly-hatched light in their filaments,
veiling their world in gauze, through which they regard
our world of crystal. Each sound, each touch
is magnified. Spiders wear their nerves
outside, in the air, their thoughts running along
the gummy, plucked strands like music.
Dark thoughts: dark, rapid music.
The trees, stone walls, wet crumbling banks, are hung
with spider-minds, revolving spiral visions
strummed in the wind. Perhaps this early sun
will bring them careless midges. The spring spiders
wait quietly for luck, one fine leg poised
to feel its tug. When it comes, it will be sudden.

* * * * *

I too: I have been spinning:
I've spread my mind out
in coils of silk, joining
stone to star, word to tree.
I stare through its threads
at all worlds, the circles
expanding, drawing in.
It seems there are doors
between them, mostly hidden.

* * * * *

What have I started? What have I set in motion?
These wheels — where will they take me? Something
is bound to happen, some shaking of the web.
I wrote my desire in wax, and transmuted it
to flame. I'm not like you, Giordano:
I'm afraid, and careful; more pliable, less fixed,
not honed to your brilliant point. You are all
swords: I'm spiderlike, labouring
in the dark, through touch, web-maker,
a bowl of water. *Spring is coming, not long now,
and then, Summer.* All our spells return on us.
Turning woman, spinning woman am I...
I can fly as high as you, for all your boasting;
and fall as hard, and make magic as lasting.

XI

TURNING NORTH

...Are we in the daylight with the light of truth rising above our horizon, or is the day with our adversaries in the antipodes?...are we in the dawn that ends the night, or in the evening of a day that is ending? *(La Cena dei Ceneri)*

Wind from the Northwest, quarter of law,
a cold just wind abseiling from the mountains,
hard flurries of hail in its skirts; in its jaws

snap glowing polar crystals, a light-show
Aurora Borealis, northern dawn. We shiver
at the season's edge, at unmistakeable omens;

knowing our scales are loaded, our coins spun
towards death. By an angled sun we see
the devastation around us, its causes known

or suspected, but we don't know what to do.
The people are powerless. Was it us who poisoned
the sea, who bulldozed and burned forests, who

gloried in war? We wanted to live, and for
that privilege became slaves. Our masters, our lords
control it all, would destroy all to hold power.

When we're facing the wrong way, we confuse
sunset and sunrise. Where's North? Where's day?
But now the Northern Lights, unfurling rose

and green, give us our bearings. Now we're sure
where the blame lies, and we're angry. All directions
become plain; and our ancestors move before

us with torches, Aurora Borealis, a banner flown
sky-high. We won't wait for justice:
we'll take it, we'll wield it, a thrown

hunting-spear, a sword. Remember, the lords are few
and frightened. There's danger: this could be
the last waving light before dark — what can we lose?

XII

THE DIVINING-BOWL

Water in its proper place is not heavy, and is not a burden to the
beings that are in the depths of the sea.   (*La Cena dei Ceneri*)

My face hanging in water
is not my face, but another's
looking down at me through hooded lids
serene, stern, secretive. A New World
face, high-cheekboned, solid-mouthed:
not mine. I recoil, disturbed,
and water slides aside, rocking my head.

Somewhere deep in the house a clock
knocks its unhurried heart.
A black iron cooking-pot
sits cold on my lap for a showstone
to see by. A gypsy's crystal
might stir suspicion; mirrors
reflect too exactly. I shall use
plain, innocent water. I breathe
the surface still, and wait.

That face suspended in darkness
swings over me. I am pulled
towards it: I feel cool rising
water breath. Blood's running
to my brain, my ears are ringing,
my chest tightens. It floats,
a mask of polished wood, the face
of an old god, giving nothing
away. And it fades, as I know it should

while the water turns cloudy and dense, becomes air.
Now pictures may appear;
I know the summoning-words, though my mouth's
too stiff to shape them. I just stare
through space till my eyes sting.

Blinking, I spoil the spell; the head
reappears, the head in the well
that will not prophesy. It swims
in its element, patient, seeing the world
from its own, altered place. "Show me
my future", I whisper

but there's only smoky water,
the weight of cold iron on my knee.

XIII

ASH WEDNESDAY

(Frankfurt, 1591)

We see how this man, as a citizen and servant of the world, a child
of Father Sun and Mother Earth, because he loves the world
too much, must be hated, censured, persecuted and extinguished
by it. But, in the meantime, may he not be idle or badly employed
while awaiting his death, his transmigration, his change...

(*Spaccio:* dedication to Sir Philip Sidney)

It's an old story, and I'm tired of it.
The bishop commissions a *memento mori*
in smooth Italian marble, employs a sculptor
to chisel a cadaver — stretched raw mouth,
collapsed eyeballs, neck like a throttled chicken,
empty and rotting cheeks, grotesque claw hands
over sunken belly — for the embittered bishop
to gaze upon and know the face of death.
The face of death! The plague still rages
here, in the backstreets: from crumbling walls
rats flicker in and out of sight as common
as children. On the cathedral steps a woman
sits with her dying child. Their presence offends
his reverence: he gives orders
to move them elsewhere. He'd prefer
to contemplate the ghastly dissolution
of his own flesh in marble, while the avoidable
small deaths crowd at his door.

How wretched to be poor in a town like this
full of beauties, full of books:
in a world like this, full of wonders.

73

When we've built our City of Light, the world
will abolish greed and hunger; yes,
it's possible, if we wish it. And death
will be respected, neither ignored nor wooed
in fascinated terror like a woman,
with careful rituals concealing fear
guilt and disgust. Death will be known
for what it is, making-new, a clean broom
sweeping the way for life, rearranging us
in shelves and corners of the universe

and I shall be dust, flying up, a billion glittering
mica-dots in the sun, one with the angels.

You will breathe me in, play in my shadows,
dip me in ink, turn my pages,
weave all my colours, fan me to flame

dance to my pattern. I shall swim
in moon-lakes of silver
watching the full earth rise.
I shall speak with the solar creatures
wading through fiery meadows: shall be
the sun too, in its splendour.
Perhaps I'll sleep in stone a million years
to be cut out like a diamond
my ashes pressed into light.

Here are my new books: figures fresh
from my mind. *On the Minimum*
(about beginnings, causes, the smallest

elements, atoms of atoms); *On Immensity*
(the Infinite Universe, the limitless,
the republics of all worlds); *On the Number One*
(about growth from tiny to huge, about Creation:
magic, faith, imagining). They're all truthful,
they'll survive me. A better monument
than this pornographic statue of despair,
these beggars at the door. It's not death I fear
the breaking-down of my tissues, the great change,
but forgetfulness. To lose
all my mind, all my labours, all
my animated pictures to age or pain —
that's the face of death I turn from,
the empty cowl. *Prega per noi
peccatori, adesso, e nell'ora...*

East wind searching my bones; a grudging Lent
starts here. God! This is a cold country.

XIV

ALCHEMY

We are in a state of continual transformation: fresh atoms are continually being reincorporated in us, while others that we received beforehand escape from us.   (*De l'Infinito*)

Wonderful what will come out of darkness:
stars, owl voices, sleep;

water, green shoots, bird's eggs
with their own curved darkness;

gemstones; a whole and perfect child
from my unseen recesses; delight

from behind shut lids, finding each other,
fingers and tongues made delicate by night.

Great magic's performed after sunset.

Old alchemists conjuring angels,
witches dancing spirals under the moon;

drum-shamans, their spirit journeys;
three nights in a tomb

staging a resurrection. Transformations
taking place out of ordinary sight.

Daylight gives us boundaries, fixes
everything. The world separates
into colours and chemicals, figures

and faces. Surfaces appear solid
reliable, unconfused. We can see
to operate complex machinery.
Only darkness permits mixing

of elements, stirring of essences
in secret, combing dark and bright

into new patterns while we sleep; so dawn
finds us transformed, shifted.

Star-particles link us with trees
dolphins and stones, travel through us

creating the universe. Base matter

becomes gold: in the Cauldron
of Annwn, in the crucible of mind

we're all magicians. The Hidden Stone,
Elixir of Life, eludes us; we've lost

the art of working through touch
with invisible forces: but as darkness

rises, and we grope wildly, perhaps
out of chaos the magic will come right.

XV

TRIUMPHANT BEAST

I do not believe in being tied, for I am certain that all the laces and
tags in the world would not suffice for that purpose.

(Eroici Furori: Intro)

The double-bolted door. That fool Mocenigo,
traitor, ape, he-goat, donkey, gigolo,
dog's turd, is out to betray me. He's thrown
my teachings at my face, knowledge hard won
in loneliness, given in good faith, paid for in trust
between friends — so I thought — spat on, crushed.

May his eyes rot, may his tongue swell and choke him:
may stinking weeping pustules break out on his skin...
My fists ache with hammering, my mouth's dry
with curses — it's hopeless; I'm trapped by my enemy,
and I'm the fool, the blind one. I believed
I was free, no chains could bind me, wings up my sleeves.

The moon flaps at my window: my mind's too full
for sleep. Surely truth will save me, my trained will,
my powers. It's an ill wind, perhaps, an opportunity.
But a crinkled edge of terror still licks at me,
a wicked, singing flame. I've had this dream before.
Now I wait for the night raid, the knock on the door.

XVI

THE STORM

Then the Triumphant Beast is driven out; that is the vices which
predominate and oppose the divine part of us.

(Lo Spaccio della Bestia Trionfante)

May the Chains of fear
May the implacable Walls of ignorance
May the Dungeon of despair
May the Battlements of violence
Fall, fall, fall, shatter
Scatter into dust shards,
Settle into molecules of earth
Fecund, forgiving, living earth

And the Rack of nightmares
The whitehot Pincers of cruelty
The Electrodes of insane power
Be smashed forever; the Warheads
Of frantic obsession, the Poisons
Of untrammelled greed, the Daggers
Of famine be thrown aside,

Be gone, be banished from us
For all time, the Jackboots of tyranny
The Noose of superstition, the Bludgeon
Of contempt, the Laboratory
Of arrogance, the Parliament of lies.
May they be powerless, futile, flicker-out
Into original darkness, be unmade,
Dissolved, defused, neutered,
Become soil and trees again, become rain.

Thunder cracks and growls its warning. A yellow light
sweats from mean slots of sky beyond the grille.
Searing flash: an explosion of heaven, a rupture
of stretched air; and out there the rain starts
in loud, thick drops, in hurrying muttering thousands,
nailing dust to earth, hammering into the ground,
spurting in noisy channels, chiming off metal,
smoking off roofs and cobbles, pumping up sound.
Each drop is a phial of scent breaking, releasing
essence of leafwater and stone, tree rubbings,
exhalations of flowers, a sea-tang. Even here, the smell
of crushed mountain herbs. My heart lifts and grows
like a shoot splitting open, drinking cloud water
in thankful, long gulps. Thunder trembles
in the walls, and I am suddenly lightened
released, restored, returned to my good senses.
There's revolution in heaven, the stars are changing.

> May the Lion of courage
> May the Dragon of knowledge
> May the Daystar of cherished hopes.
> May the Moon of love
> Shine, shine on us, may we turn
> Our faces up to theirs:

> The Country of healing dreams
> (only found at the point of bliss)
> The Ocean of compassion
> The Mountain of inner power
> (and the white track up to the summer pasture)
> Be there for us, O may we walk there

In freedom, in balance, in simplicity;
And may the Cauldron of plenty
Brim over, feed the children:

May we put on justice, our Clothes
Of brilliant colours, worn openly
Danced in; may we understand
This living world, this Universe, all
Worlds, each other, respect
Life, respect Earth, our wayward
Selves; and gathering the Flowers
Of humility — not in guilt now
But innocence — run back, back to our old
Home, the forgotten land, the Garden.

Lightning arrows down, sings in the gutters, flares
to find me in my cell, rekindles my centre.
Then the thunderstorm rolls away, rolls into the hills.

* * * * * * *

"Let this not trouble you, Momus," said Isis, "since fate
has ordained a vicissitude of darkness and light."

"But the worst of it is," said Momus, "that they hold it
for certain that they are in the light..."

XVII

COSMOLOGY

The soul is not in the body: the body is in the soul. It is steeped in the soul like a net in the sea.   (*Eroici Furori*)

Stars on this high dizzy night
now my eyes are washed dark
of artificial indoor light, shine
down, down, into the measureless reaches
of the sky's ocean, layers deep
skimming aside from my hand
plunged among them. I know
without benefit of telescopic sight

the universe is not exploding out
from its centre like a bomb, a point
of ignition. The centre's everywhere,
and everywhere's expanding, not
ripping apart but sailing out
on a grand exhalation, outbreath
of life, which moves the waters
above and below, stirs weathers

and galaxies, clouds and sap,
pumping the blood around.
In this outbreath we live:
float, swim, soar, fall,
journey out and return, increase
and sparkle. After a time
there'll be a breathing-in
contraction to density, Destiny

and then out again, life again.
No, I'll not be part of a detonation,
some celestial terrorist act.
I'd rather be part of an infinite
animal, microbe of dragon-breath —
or a droplet of stupendous, thundering wave
breaking on the sands of eternity
poured out, poured out to the sky.

An image of hope displayed: a young woman rising
from the foam of the sea, who on reaching the shore
wipes off the humour of the sea with her palms....
and another image: a woman kneeling naked
in starlight by a gleaming pool, and with vessels
in either hand, from which she pours water
onto the parched land, and into the pool.

I swim in nurturing liquid, a child
in the womb of matter. The holy well
uncoils its rivers in me, its threads of light.
A taste of stone in the water, of rock,
the bones of earth. Closing my eyes, I see it,
taste, feel it; and I'm young again
and in Nola, filling stone jars with my mother
who said, Don't spill a drop, it's rare
and precious, there are stars asleep in it;
it holds their powerful rays. Dissolved
in dew, their distant fires, shaping my days.

XVIII

THE VOYAGER

Wisdom is set in our spirit, seated on the poop of our soul,
holding the tiller of the ship which it steers across the temp-
estuous sea of the century.   (*Oratio Valedictoria*)

I'm your silver, I'm your guide in the night, your dancer,
your voyager sailing the storm, your adventurer
feathered strokes dipping waterskin, a rainbow dazzle
flung out on the tips of my wings, the whisperer
in your inner ear, your deceiver, impossible sweet
changing-faced lover, your infinitely wild
passionate unrestrained your divine possessor
who rises and shines above time and reflects
the universe in your mind, the torch that shows
all your coloured images; I'm a dolphin-rider
dragging you into the sea, strange shapes in the water
rising to meet, dissolving you bone from bone, a
bitter solution, drinking you in; I'm your muse
I'm your madness, your loneliness, wanting you only
for me to play my rays on, mirror me in your eyes,
surprise and creep up behind, to find you out,
turn you round about and devour you, feed you
to the wolves, chop and change you, rearrange
your careful thoughts, circles of memory unspun
flung overboard and drowned; but plunge deep
in me, they'll be found whole and new, restored
if you trust me: I'm your last hope, your saviour
healer and teacher, your light when all lights
go out, your mariner. So follow me, take my hand,
let me sidle into your dreams, there's no need to be
afraid, I'm only the shadow, pure moonlight, look
through me and see the sun rise, the voyage made.

XIX

SOLSTICE

The Sun must move, if it is a fire, because Fire is the most mobile
of the elements. When we prevent flames from rising, when we
imprison them in the bowels of the furnace, they twist impatiently
about themselves.

(*La Cena dei Ceneri*)

Hot yellow moon rose
last night, transformed
into sun, deep gold
over intense black rustling
leaves breathing stored
green scent of long day;
so all night the sky
shone, there was no night:
the triumph of light

renewed, Summer, most fiercely
hoped-for, called up
out of strength in the cold
months, with force,
with images of lions.
Sun in glory, at
zenith, convulsed with fire;
astronomers predict
magnetic surges, solar storms,
electrical disruption, flares
leaping millions of miles.

When the transformation
comes, it will be sudden
gold forming in the crucible.

The flame erupts, it must
move, must burn, no
turning-back seasons
scuttling down nocturnal
holes; its rays penetrate
to the core of matter,
change everything. We've
reason to hope: after four
hundred mechanistic years
of dispiriting gloom

the sun breaks through,
revealing a world alive
and us at the chasm's brink
shocked, lost, amazed.

Today's warm to touch,
ripens grass, blackcurrants,
my yeasty skin. Bees
cluster and dip dark heads
into purple sage. The air
seethes, stirred by the sun.
We breathe in its ferment
it moves us from the inside;
It's a secret
process, most magical.
The world must turn
to receive dawn, to receive
Summer; and we
are the world waking up

the trees reborn
over their charred stumps
the clean seas rising.

XX

FIELD OF FLOWERS

Time takes everything and gives everything. All things change.
Nothing is destroyed forever.   (*Candelaio*)

Perhaps you are more afraid in passing this sentence than I am in
hearing it. (G. Bruno to his judges: from the *Summary* of his trial.)

It's winter out there, in the world,
in the old Field of Flowers
paved with dead stones, dusted with corpse
salts and gritty leavings, smoke-blown and sour.

Waiting for dawn, for the last
time, on my knees in the listening
dark (that has always frightened me, who
was born to see the sun) I can't stop shivering

and thinking of fire. It's my way
out of cold, out of winter, infernal
circles of this prison, which I have chosen:
to blaze like a torch, escape in a churning

column of smoke over the domes and spires
and towers and pinnacles of Rome
to be blown, blown away. Calcination,
rendering down to ash, to scorched crumbs, greasy foam:

the first degree of transformation. Out there
in the wind, in the public eye
of morning, shaven and bound and given
to the flames, I shall struggle and choke and die.

It's winter, but spring is coming,
not long now; and then — I forget:
it's too dark, the flowers are blotted-out.
Ripples of memory dwindle behind my shut

lids; statues, seals, hieroglyphs, gods
and graces falling away. I turn
like a moth in the vast night of unknowing
drawn by one light, one lovely flame that will burn

me up: one lust, one lunacy. Let me
go — I'm engulfed in her dazzling wings
taken in to the hammering heart of fire, its secrets.
From a cypress beyond the gates, dawn preens and sings.

XXI

THE DANCE

There is a continual rising and falling through the chain of the
elements...By connecting higher with lower, you have one
beautiful animal, the World.   (*De Umbris Idearum*)

1

Press your ear to the ground. Hear
buzzing through soil and nerve, the long
slow life of the Earth, its rage
and weariness. Don't be surprised:
you always knew it was so, that Earth
stored lives, deaths, memories
in its teeming cells. The thoughts of the Earth
are my thoughts. You are right to be afraid.

2

If you fly too close to the sun you'll burn;
your wings will melt, you'll fall
and the sea will swallow you. Too much light
sends you insane: the only remedy
is to hang by a foot in the dusk
with your nose to Earth, learn stillness
at the heart of the dance, the bent-
legged Kathakali posture that commands
attention. Bruno, you soared, you flew
crazy rejoicing lover of the world, and the world
upset, upended you. Now through closed
eyes, through dreams, your night-fears
vanished, through poems, through touch
in darkness you feel your way back, lit only

fitfully by the moon. Now your voice is
the voice of Earth, which we strain to hear.

3

Spinning translucent jewel
falling back into night,
point of light in the caverns
of fire-gems, with its life-blue
its spiral of winds:
we don't surmise, we know
we belong to a star, a famous
luminary. We are the Heavens
the Firmament, the angelic realm
glimpsed from great airless spaces;
here is Paradise, the Garden,
our only home, the shining
City, Adocentyn in all colours
and images, the World
that was always there but mostly
invisible, turning and changing
changing us, whether we will
or no: and inside it's burning.

4

Dancing the wild atomic reel
The Old Wheels of the World, a tune
Taught us, it's said, by the fairies —

Shiva's dance in his ring of flames —
Life came through the cosmic gates

Weaving its nets, its sidesteps

Its chancy patterns. Science rests
On illusions, reflections, shadows
Of lifting footsteps, echoes of half

Heard music. Caught in the dance
We can't stop to analyse, but must
Learn to love dancing, moved by inner

Drumming, swung rhythms begun
By our ancient Mother the Sea.
At the hub of her web, the Spider also

Dances, draws cords from her body, circles
Outwards then winds them in
To the spool of herself, the World

Pulled out, drawn back by those threads
Which we all spin, webwork of memory
And Love. In the well, the womb-waters

Our future multiplies, particles of soul
Dance through the elements, and I take
The hands of all my loves, and we begin.

Now I understand, I understand everything.

Notes on the Poems

TWO RIVERS

The Sealwife

There is a story from Scotland about a fisherman who takes a wife from among the seal people. He watches them dance by moonlight, and steals one of their sealskins and hides it in the rocks. When dawn approaches, the sealfolk hurry back into their sealskins and return to the sea, except for one young woman whose skin it is that was stolen. Regretfully, her people leave her on the shore, and the fisherman carries her off to live with him. She becomes his wife and bears him several children, but she always longs to return to her own people. One day, the children come running in from the beach. One of them has something he has found in the rocks: her old sealskin. She pulls it on, says a sorrowful farewell to her children, and swims out to sea. It is said that she sometimes returned to speak with them from the safety of a rock a little way from the shore; but she never set foot on land again.

Breakfast with the Poets

The city of Almería in South-eastern Spain was the centre of an ancient Moorish kingdom. In its heyday in the 11th century AD it was famous throughout Europe as an important port for trade with North Africa, and was noted for its astoundingly beautiful weaving; and also for its poets. It was one of the last cities in Spain to fall to the Catholics, and the only one to have been shelled by the Nazis. Since the Catholic Reconquest in the 15th century Almería has been in a slow decline, and only now with tourism steadily encroaching eastward from the Costa del Sol is the city again beginning to expand. Almería is my maternal grandfather's city: he was born in the village of Oanes in the Alpujarra mountains to the north-west, in the fertile valley of the river Andarax (now decimated by drought).

Almería is still noted for its poets, and while visiting with my family I attended a poetry reading at dawn in the Moorish fortress, the Alcazaba above the town. The reading included Moorish music and dance, and a *desayuno* of herb tea, fruit and 'Moorish' cakes afterwards. The event was to celebrate a famous Almerían poet: Al-Mutasim Ibn Sumadih, king of Almería in the late 11th century. Contemporary poets read from his work in Spanish, and also from their own work.

...See, I have laid... This is my translation of an extract from one of Mutasim's poems, translated into Spanish by Amelina Ramon Guerrero, Professor of Arabic Studies at the University of Granada.

BOOK OF SHADOWS

Giordano Bruno was born in Nola, southern Italy, in 1548 and was burnt at the stake in Rome in 1600. He became famous in his early twenties, while still in his monastery in Naples, as an outstanding practitioner of the *Ars Memoriae* or Art of Memory. This was an ancient and complex mnemoic system, in which one imagined a room and peopled it with the facts one wished to remember in the form of symbolic objects around the room. So when you wanted to recall a specific fact, you merely entered your imaginary room, remembering on which chair or in which alcove or on which windowsill that fact was perched, and there it was waiting for you, in whatever graphic and stunning form you had invested it. The memory room could be expanded as need arose, to become a cathedral or palace or memory theatre of whatever subtle or intricate design you chose, provided it was logical, and thereby easily committed to memory. It is said of Bruno that he soon ran out of places to house all the things he wished to remember (because he wished to remember all the knowledge of the world). So he asked his superiors if it was permissible to travel in his imagination beyond the Earth and its spheres to the stars and the heavens. The answer was no; it was not permissible: but he did so anyway, in the quest for other worlds in which to place his thoughts. And that is how he began his dangerous speculations on astronomy and the true nature of the Universe. Well, it makes a good story.

Bruno was a prolific writer during his short career, and many of his writings are in the form of poetry. He spent a couple of years in England (1583–6) and became a well-known figure at the court of Elizabeth I. During his English exile he wrote several of his most interesting works, including his great poetic treatise *De Gli Eroici Furori* (On Heroic Frenzy) which he dedicated to his good friend Sir Philip Sidney. Both Bruno and Sidney had close links with Welsh magician Dr. John Dee and his circle. Bruno had a Scottish disciple called Dicson who did a lot to popularise his philosophy in Britain. There is evidence, too, that Shakespeare knew of Bruno and his teachings and may have been influenced by them (see F. Yates: *Giordano Bruno and the Hermetic Tradition*, ch. XIX). In fact, the name of Giordano Bruno was notorious throughout Europe.

He continued to be an important influence on non-Establishment thought until about the middle of the 17th century, when the new scientific rationalism finally triumphed.

The main thrust of his philosophy, which had its roots in the ancient world and its branches in the new learning of the Renaissance, was (briefly) this:

—That Nature is alive, and that all life is animated from within, not from any outer force. Matter and Spirit are indivisible, and Matter is divine.

—All life-forms are inter-related and formed from the same basic ingredients; therefore we should respect all forms of life.

—That the Universe is infinite, and contains innumerable worlds. (He found the vast scale of the Universe joyful and heartening rather than fearful and depressing.) That there are also infinite possibilities for change in the world.

—The supreme importance of the Poet in society (on a par with the Magus), as someone able to *change* and *shape* events as well as to reflect and comment on them.

—The need to turn to alternative, non-Christian beliefs and cultures for the creative wisdom to balance our dominant world-view.

—The possibility of a better, juster society, and our duty to strive to improve social justice.

—Sexual love, religious ecstasy, poetic inspiration and intellectual vision are all expressions of one divine 'heroic frenzy', which is the creative urge that gives birth to the Universe.

For these beliefs, and for his avowed intentions to replace the Christianity of those times with a new religion based on creative magic, Bruno was burnt to death on the Campo de'Fiori in Rome after eight years' imprisonment in the dungeons of the Inquisition.

Bruno was brought up in Aristotle's universe of fixed elements and starry spheres, with Heaven above and beyond it all, and Hell somewhere deep in the Earth — that lowliest object furthest removed from God. His realisation —

however he came by it — that the vision was false, that the Earth is no more at the centre than anywhere else is, that the rigid circles of existence culminating in Heaven were an illusion, the Universe in fact being infinitely vast with innumerable stars and planets; that realisation gave him an exhilarating sense of release that we find hard to imagine nowadays. Perhaps it was all too much for him. Perhaps it sent him mad: he certainly suffered from some strange delusions (The Pope would listen to his ideas and welcome them... Singlehandedly, the Nolan would change the world...). But it was a creative madness all the same; the madness of a poet. It is this poet's excitement that spills out into his writing, making it more than philosophy or even mere magical esoterics. Without the poetic fire, the 'Heroic Frenzy', it would be obscure and unreadable today. Yet Bruno's story and his strange ideas continue to capture our imaginations, those of us who are rebels at heart, poets at heart.

There is another important strand in these poems, as important (so it's turned out) as Giordano Bruno himself, though I confess that wasn't my original intention.

I needed a structure to work to, one that suited the general atmosphere of Bruno's ideas and times, which would be relevant to my own experience too. So I chose the Tarot, a collection of symbols in pictorial form, familiar to me and surely familiar to Bruno as well. A common point of reference, perhaps. These days the cards are used chiefly for fortune telling, but they have other uses too. I like to look at the pictures and think about what they symbolise, treat them as visual metaphors, rich sources of imagery.

Each poem in the sequence has a relationship to one of the 22 cards of the Major Trumps of the Tarot. The relationship varies from tenuous (e.g. *The Inner Artificer*) to fairly direct (*Cosmology*). The poems are numbered according to the usual numbering of the Tarot Trumps, from 0 to 21, and they match the usual order of the cards.

I first became interested in Bruno through reading a novel: a strange, rich novel by the American author John Crowley, called *Little, Big*. His next novel, *Aegypt*, features Bruno much more directly, through the device of a book within a book (one of the many books within that book). Because of the glimpses in Crowley's books of something mysterious and compelling, I wanted to know more, and I found scholarly works that made my head spin. But I felt I was on the edge of discovering, or rediscovering, something quite simple and familiar. So I wanted to go further in, and as a poet, it seemed to

me that the way in was through poetry; and Bruno was a poet too. And that is
how these poems began.

Tarot Correspondences

0	THE FOOL	(Nola)
I	THE MAGICIAN	(Book of Shadows)
II	THE HIGH PRIESTESS	(Athene)
III	THE EMPRESS	(The Inner Artificer)
IV	THE EMPEROR	(Conjuration)
V	THE HIEROPHANT/POPE	(The Art Of Memory)
VI	THE LOVERS	(Heroic Frenzy)
VII	THE CHARIOT	(The Journey)
VIII	STRENGTH	(Sun In Leo)
IX	THE HERMIT	(In Aegypt)
X	THE WHEEL OF FORTUNE	(The Revolving Castle)
XI	JUSTICE	(Turning North)
XII	THE HANGED MAN	(The Divining-Bowl)
XIII	DEATH	(Ash Wednesday)
XIV	TEMPERANCE	(Alchemy)
XV	THE DEVIL	(Triumphant Beast)
XVI	THE TOWER	(The Storm)
XVII	THE STAR	(Cosmology)
XVIII	THE MOON	(The Voyager)
XIX	THE SUN	(Solstice)
XX	JUDGEMENT	(Field of Flowers)
XXI	THE WORLD	(The Dance)

Nola

Nola was Bruno's birthplace, a town in the Campagna of Southern Italy, within
sight of Mt. Vesuvius.

"our green mountain": Monte Cicala, Nola's local hill.

"bee-swarms in the earth": this alludes to the phenomenon called the
Hummadruz, of unknown origin, that is occasionally experienced on hot
windless days, especially on hilltops or around ancient sites.

Book of Shadows

Modern occultists often refer to their personal books of ritual or magical diaries as their *Book of Shadows*. Most are unaware that the term was popularised by the success of Bruno's first published work *De Umbris Idearum* (On the Shadows of Ideas), a treatise on magical conjuration and astrology. This, together with Cornelius Agrippa's *Occult Philosophy*, was secretly read by many would-be conjurers, at great danger to themselves, as possession of these books was considered proof of diabolical heresy. As late as the 19th century in Brittany, many country folk kept a book of spells, usually chained and padlocked, known as an *Agrippa*. It was thought dangerous for anyone other than the village priest to make use of an *Agrippa* (see Derek Bryce: *The Celtic Legend of the Beyond*). In other parts of France and in England such spellbooks were sometimes known as a *Book of Shadows*.

The image of a broken mirror in the first stanza comes from *Lamps of the Thirty Statues*. In the poems that follow, I have occasionally borrowed from Bruno's prolific and often startling imagery.

Athene

In the opening quotation (from a farewell speech given at the University of Wittenburg) Bruno is referring to Minerva the Goddess of Wisdom (Athene in Greece), whose emblem was an owl. The owl motif can be traced back to prehistoric 'Eye Goddess' representations.

The Inner Artificer

This poem arose from a photograph of a transgenic pig developed by genetic scientists at the US Dept. of Agriculture, Beltsville, Maryland. The pig had been implanted with human growth gene. It grew quickly to a huge size, but was blind, excessively hairy, sterile, and crippled with arthritis. The monster's creators considered Pig 6707 a great scientific advance. The poem's title is from a statement of Bruno's concerning Nature as the creative power of the Universe: *Da noi si chiama artifice interna*. This phrase is translated at the beginning of stanza 3. Every other statement in that stanza is also taken directly from Bruno.

The Journey

Adocentyn was first described in a mediaeval Spanish/Arabic book of magic called *Picatrix* (a book of terrifying reputation), as a marvellous city built by Hermes Trismegistus, the mythical founder of alchemy and magical lore. Adocentyn was situated "in the east of Egypt" and was twelve miles long, and contained speaking statues and a great tree "which bore the fruit of all generation". It also contained a tower with a lighthouse rotating in seven colours, one for each day of the week. Images placed around the city walls helped to make the inhabitants virtuous and to protect them from harm. Many Renaissance philosophers were inspired by Adocentyn to propose similar Utopian cities or states, based on harnessing beneficial supernatural forces (see F Yates: *Giordano Bruno and the Hermetic Tradition*).

Sun in Leo

A talismanic poem, summoning the virtue of Strength or Fortitude. The tarot card *Strength* generally depicts a woman with a lion in a desert landscape. Its equivalent among the suit cards, The Queen of Wands, shows an enthroned woman surrounded by sunflowers with cats at her feet.

In Aegypt

To understand exactly what I mean by the term "Aegypt" (as opposed to Egypt), you will have to read John Crowley's novel of that title. In the meantime, Crowley's suggestion is that there were two "Egypts" in the ancient world: the historical Egypt of the Pharoahs, and another Egypt, a country of the imagination, whose borders may, or may not, have touched the "real" Egypt — a mysterious region from which came all magical arts and skills, a shadow country of great wisdom that was in some ways like Egypt but "not Egypt, not Egypt at all...but Aegypt" (John Crowley: *Aegypt* pp 99–102). The real Egypt we now know to have been a fairly barbarous place, with a tyrannical state based on slavery and a grotesque, deathbound religion, materialistic and superstitious. Yet throughout the Middle Ages and even up to the present day, Egypt has been revered as the source of great civilisation and arcane wisdom, a magnet for romantic imaginings. Egypt has been confused with Aegypt: and Aegypt has fallen, with her secret doctrines, her harmonious religion of life (not death), her wise women and men, all barely more than a legend, fragmented and scattered.

For the alchemists and hermetic philosophers such as Bruno, some of the old Tale and teachings of Aegypt were preserved in a collection of writings, the *Corpus Hermeticum*, once thought to be older than Moses, but discovered in the 17th century to date from the 2nd century AD. These mysterious and beautiful writings from the last years of Paganism were an inspiration to Bruno: he continually quotes from them or alludes to them. It was his belief that Aegypt could be restored and its truths revealed, its "religion of the world" returned to, to the betterment of human society. That was his mission, his Great Work, to be accomplished through magic and poetry.

"O Aegypt, Aegypt": from the *Corpus Hermeticum*; the "Lament for the Egyptian Religion".

In my poem, Aegypt is a region of dreams and of ecstasy, the place where everything becomes clearly understood. We help each other to discover it, through sharing knowledge, and also through sexual passion, the sharing of delight. The idea being that Aegypt is an integral part of each of us, our hidden potential, our powers to transform.

The Revolving Castle

The title is a translation of *Caer Sidi*, the castle of the Celtic Goddess Arianrhod, ruler of the turning heavens (and therefore of Fate). One of her emblems was the Spider. Arianrhod means "Silver Wheel", another image of the constellations.

Turning North

"quarter of law": according to Native American tradition, each compass direction has a symbolic meaning or "medicine" — hence the "Medicine Wheel". In the Medicine Wheel the North West is the direction of Law, meaning natural law, and the morality of nature that says "as you sow, so shall you reap", the Law of Returns. The restoration of *law* (a society based on natural justice) was a recurring theme of Bruno's.

"Remember, the lords are few": here is a nod, a respectful and admiring nod, in the direction of Ursula K. Le Guin's *City of Illusions*.

100

Ash Wednesday

"Prega per noi/peccatori": from the Italian *Hail Mary* — "pray for us sinners, now, and at the hour (of our death)".

Triumphant Beast

Zuan Mocenigo, a wealthy Venetian, invited Bruno to his house in 1592, to learn from him the secrets of the Art of Memory. After Bruno had stayed with him for about two months, Mocenigo became alarmed at the extent of the Nolan's heresies, and refused to allow him to return to Germany. He locked Bruno in his room and denounced him to the Inquisition, who dragged him from his bed in the early hours of May 26th 1592. As Frances Yates observes: "On that day began for Bruno eight years of imprisonment ending in death".

The Storm

The incantatory sections are inspired by Bruno's extraordinary conjuration for "the Reform of the Heavens" in *Lo Spaccio della Bestia Trionfante* (The Expulsion of the Triumphant Beast).

"Let this not trouble you, Momus": this snatch of dialogue is also from *Spaccio*.

Solstice

"The Sun must move":Bruno believed, with Copernicus, that the Earth and other planets moved round the Sun. But his speculations went way beyond Copernicus, some of them fantastically wild (such as assuming intelligent life-forms on every heavenly body, including the Sun), and some surprisingly accurate (such as his explanation for the motion of the Earth and the fluctuation of seasons). He thought the Sun must turn on its axis *because it is a fire, and Fire is mobile*; he thought the Earth "wobbled" on its axis, producing the seasons *because the Earth in its wisdom wanted to bring the benefits of sunlight to all its parts* — this shows how very differently his mind worked from that of conventional astronomers.

Field of Flowers

Bruno was burnt alive in the Campo de Fiori in Rome on February 17th 1600. Several witnesses testified to his death. This Roman square was the site of countless horrible executions. Strangely enough, while I was writing these poems I noticed a car advertisement in one of the Sunday colour supplements that was set in the Campo de Fiori. On the damp cobbles of the square was a bright red car, and under the square's name was a smart *gelateria* offering Visa facilities. How times have changed!

The Dance

"The thoughts of the Earth": from a Navajo Indian chant

It is lovely indeed, it is lovely indeed:
I, I am the spirit within the Earth.
The feet of the Earth are my feet;
The legs of the Earth are my legs;
The strength of the Earth is my strength;
The voice of the Earth is my voice;
The thoughts of the Earth are my thoughts;
The feather of the Earth is my feather.
All that belongs to the Earth belongs to me;
All that surrounds the Earth surrounds me;
For I, I am the sacred words of the Earth:
It is lovely indeed, it is lovely indeed.

"I belong to a star, a famous luminary": G. Bruno: *De Immenso IV. The Old Wheels of the World* is the title of an Irish reel, one of the many traditional tunes reputed to have come to humankind from the fairies.